THE EIGHTH MOUNTAIN
POETRY PRIZE

THE EIGHTH MOUNTAIN POETRY PRIZE was held first
annually and then biennially for a decade from 1988 to
1998. *Friction* was selected by Naomi Shihab Nye and is the
final volume. Other volumes in the series are:

The Eating Hill
Karen Mitchell
SELECTED BY AUDRE LORDE
$8.95

Fear of Subways
Maureen Seaton
SELECTED BY MARILYN HACKER
$9.95

Cultivating Excess
Lori Anderson
SELECTED BY JUDY GRAHN
$9.95

Between the Sea and Home
Almitra David
SELECTED BY LINDA HOGAN
$10.95

The Humming Birds
Lucinda Roy
SELECTED BY LUCILLE CLIFTON
$12.95

FRICTION

Claire Bateman

THE EIGHTH MOUNTAIN PRESS

PORTLAND • OREGON • 1998

Cover design by Marcia Barrentine
Book design by Ruth Gundle
Cover art by Mary Josephson, "For Those Who Choose to Live"

First American Edition, 1998
1 2 3 4 5 6 7 8 9
Printed in the United States

The Eighth Mountain Press wishes to express sincere gratitude to Oregon Literary Arts, Inc., for financial support that helped to make possible the publication of Friction.

LIBRARY OF CONGRESS CATALOGING-IN-PUBLICATION DATA
Bateman, Claire.
    Friction / Claire Bateman.
        p.   cm.
    ISBN 0-933377-48-7 (tradepaper : alk. paper)
    ISBN 0-933377-49-5 (lib. bdg. : alk. paper)
    I. Title.
    PS3552.A826884F75 1998
    811'.54--dc21   98-42513

The Eighth Mountain Press
624 Southeast 29th Avenue
Portland, Oregon 97214
phone: 503/233-3936
fax: 503/233-0774

ACKNOWLEDGMENTS

Some of the poems in this book were previously published as follows:

Charlotte Poetry Review: "Wholes"

Cream City Review: "Bed" and "Yes"

Eleventh Muse: "Life on Earth"

Emrys: "Damage Assessment"

45/96: The Ninety-Six Sampler of South Carolina Poetry: "Leeuwenhoek: Delft, 1740," "Life on Earth," and "Movers"

Georgia Review: "Pluck"

Kenyon Review: "Character" and "Milk"

Louisiana Literature: "Blue"

Nebraska Review: "Body Work" and "Pure"

New England Review: "Friction" and "Sky"

New Virginia Review: "Sugar"

Paris Review: "Hair," "Stitching the Bride," and "Ectoplasm"

Passages North: "Gloves"

Poetry Daily: "Blessing Song"

Poetry Miscellany: "Prehistoric Mother"

Pushcart Prize Special Mention: "Gloves"

Southern Review: "Waiting for Red"

Taos Review: "Horses" and "Tracking"

Third Coast: "Under Water in the Orthopedic Waiting Room" and "Blessing Song"

I would like to thank the National Endowment for the Arts and the Tennessee Arts Commission for grants which enabled me to complete this collection.

CONTENTS

I. BODY WORK

II. THE AUTODIDACT:
THE INTIMATE RECOLLECTIONS & REFLECTIONS
OF FRANKENSTEIN'S CREATURE

III. DAMAGE ASSESSMENT

IV. SHADOW PLAY

Body Work

Tracking

At last the rudimentary lovers moved
closer, face to face,
not knowing what came next,
lips touching as if
of their own accord
in variation that was neither
eating nor suckling,
but some third thing
that included and excluded both,
as demanding as it was
faintly repugnant, & *the kiss* leapt
into the synapses of their brains.

I hope the recording angels
noted this in that console
on which actions are registered,
where they could watch the kiss
leaping oceans, a small
brightness sparking across the screen,
each sequence & design transposed
into music to be sung
impartially, preserved,
as monks in the Dark Ages
preserved knowledge.

Life on Earth

Mostly, it was about
eating, & being,
food. Everyone
came & stayed
for epochs.
Translucent worms
pushed the annual
eighteen tons of earth
through crop & gizzard.
Ants milked captive aphid herds,
stroking their sides
to coax the sticky fluid.
The octopus perfected its monotonous
embrace & release,
& the starfish turned
its stomach inside out. The snake
opened its hinged jaws
as if yawning.
After awhile, someone
invented the family,
forks, romance,
& related culinary fantasies.
In retrospect,
it wasn't unlike dreaming.
You could even say it had
a kind of sweetness—
everything about to become
something else, taking
its time; yes,

it was hunger
that made the world
go 'round,
& on the good days
we could love
how it needed us
terribly as a child:
always naked, never
at fault, the best
we would ever
leave behind.

Body Work

A foreign object can remain in the stomach
for years, the soft tissue growing together
around the edges until it disappears. Spoons
enough to swamp a bridal
register. Dimes, pens, miniature
transistors. For every hand
chewed up by the Safeway grinder,
you could count dozens of AA batteries
corroded by the gut's wet love.
Through babies, crazies, & the rare
vocational swallowers, things find
their way in. All these
the night janitor rescues
from O.R. and the big metal dumpsters
behind the morgue. For years
he's been weaving them
with lengths of wire retrieved
from the alimentary canal. His personal
favorite: incisors, canines, molars, fused
into one misshapen grinning jaw, so
when the right wind slams
down the alley to his back yard,
it chatters, percussion
for the humming sinews
and reed tones of the flute
mouthpiece caught forever
in the creature's throat.
What arpeggios his outcast strains for
in the variable weathers of the larger world.

Everything inside wants to get out;
everything outside wants to get in—but
it cannot sing.

Leeuwenhoek: Delft, 1740

Does he ever lose the tremor in coming up?
That brief near-pain as his eye releases *the animalcules*
whose motion is so swift, & so various,
upwards, downwards, & round about,
that 'tis wonderful to see the windings & turnings,
extension & contradiction lit in the dark field
beneath the lens he'd ground & polished
through eyestrain, headache,
the muscles of the hand rebelling
in tiny spasms, a slight contained vertigo his only passport.

Impatient with fatigue & blur, he rests his gaze
beyond his window on some middle distance,
& there it is, the world going on without him:
chimney smoke, merchants, dogs,
their forms pouring in on floods of light
as he throws open the casement to gulp salt wind.
He has not until now been aware of the notional fact
that it is spring, though he has for weeks crouched in mud
to tenderly seek the seed-buds & the first weeds to be brought
through the narrow crafted tunnel toward sight.

After his death they will find the 247 microscopes
mounted in gold, in silver, & in brass,
& the pages crowded with fine script.
Globules of Blood from which its Redness proceeds,
Crystalline Humour from the Eye of a Whale,
all evaporated, like the treasures recovered
from the mouth of a neighbor who had never cleaned his teeth.

Confess it, life's pulp is obsession,
despite the townsfolk & their stolid wives
who do not want to know what dangles
on their eyelashes, what breeds in each crevice
of their bodies & their bodies' houses,
who demand that the world be all solidity & simple movement,
as if nothing can be trusted but the concentrated local force
of each propulsion, the hand a hand only, the eye an eye,
not a globe with its own life violent in waters.
They will not descend into smallness, into his invisible realm
which is not only real, but the future, teeming.
Confidently lonely, he leans out
to salute the tops of their wide hats.

Walking

I see my neighbors every evening.
Their nods & smiles prove
they see me too. We should be
stubs by now, worn down by concrete
through sneakers & padded socks, ankles & shins,
into a nub of trunk, a smudge of head; we should be
thumblings hiding in upholstery
from our children who haven't begun to shrink,
are not diminished yet by sidewalk, the chosen
route to work, & by the pillow
where the face moves back and forth in sleep,
twisting off sheets of skin. It must be
food that saves us, the dinners we now are walking off,
the deaths of animals raised toward such an end,
the smaller deaths of plants steamed or sauteed,
salted, lifted by forkful every night
into their afterlife, their walking heaven.

Wholes

Why can't I do addition in my head?
The instant my attention skips
backward to the lefthand number,
the first vanishes down the rabbit hole
they all eventually lie
at the bottom of, twisted & bleeding, still
conscious it's all my fault if one's
to blame for mental inadequacies;
or are such defects responsible
for the soul, like the gifts
offered by the bad
fairies at a storychild's cradle?
Nor can I think to shop
for items more than one no matter
how related, milk and eggs
I drop so often they must secretly
incite the breakage
that is their only surety
of release, not wishing to be
abandoned in my refrigerator for weeks
til they're ignobly
discarded. So I was happy
when the bag was invented,
little sack of skin tied
at the top with sinew,
modeled after various internal organs,
& no one yet fully
aware of this brand new idea's radiance:
removable contents, soul-

organization, & a little later,
the list, inside-out flattened
pouch of representations,
memory's Mercator, subject
to distortions, elaborations,
the most exquisite shorthands, there being no
motivation toward self-
gathering in objects themselves.
Everything speaks
of attrition: secret scabs,
dim moods, gossip layers,
marriages. Rusting on the margins
of one parkway alone,
the tagged cars I count
could become their own
city. Pull the cord tight
around this month's stacked-up news.
Blow the clogged hairs
from the shaver head.
Sweep the condoms out
from under the bed, pale
lolling winded balloons.
With each step, we lose
ten thousand flecks of skin.
Yet still we arrive from the inside
out, raining down as the world
accumulates in our wake.

Waiting for Red

One of those delicate
arrangements. He had
to practice to get it
right—the small
bustling steps, the voice,
the grandmotherly
inflections. He needed
her help, her directions,
though he was what they call
in that line of work
a quick study.
She in his belly clapped
her plump white hands.
Hadn't she always
dreamed of a little
extra speed, a certain
impropriety?
In the dark, she closed
her eyes & gave herself up
to muscle rhythms & the remembered
scent of streams along the timberline,
the remembered scent of blood.
In himself he recognized
a certain suppressed
domesticity: slant
of light through lace
curtains, weight of quietness
on that kind of afternoon.
They could have played

all day like that
but for the arrival
of the child,
always the child,
unable to tolerate
ambiguities. So difficult
the resolution, chroniclers
can't agree. He was slit
tail to throat by that
woodcutter of the precise
distinctions.
Or no, he merely
coughed her up & loped away.
She irritable now who used to be
so *sweet*. He skulking past
dress shops, fighting a lust
for tea.

Sugar

You of the night
light, white
tiles, & house
slippers: run
for it, chase
your daughters
shrieking to the car
& drive
hard, leaning
on your horn the whole
half-mile, peel in
to Quik Save, leave them
strapped, tracking you
through glass
as you flap down the aisles.
Home, you pop
your paper bag
like a piñata; time
to teach
the girls to cheat
for Hershey's Kiss,
Starburst, Milky Way,
the high stakes
of the morally slack.
Shuffle,
& let those empty
calories click in
like zeros: malto-
dextrin, soy lecithin,
vanillin—hurry,

Queen Frostine,
before it's too late
for them to learn
the monoglyceride
rag, bite & spit
the tops of small
wax bottles, get drunk
on blue elixir,
your oldest in the pink
pajama top
stacking the deck,
the youngest in the bottoms
with the spare
ace stuck to her spine
by sweat—let
them fall
asleep where they
sprawl in a waste
of foil balls,
their hair
spiked in sticky clumps,
their lips coated
with sugar. Now,
softly,
here come the ants
in single file—
Puritans
all, this once
they will march
their clean
dotted lines
around you, taking
just what they want
for free.

Milk

For years, he assumed they were always full, milk
everywhere, invisible under dresses; impossibly close
as he swayed for balance in busses; heating up
at the beach inside Spandex bikinis; sloshing a little
with sudden motion—one of those things in life
you just get used to. No doubt women spoke of it
privately to each other in complicated female code
on days when it bothered them, if it bothered them,
so that all around him, without his ever hearing,
milk-speech blossomed in lovely euphemism.
Not until he moved in with his second sweetheart
did he figure it out. He thought it best not to tell her.
Now he knows they're mostly empties.
They don't feel any different to the touch.
He can't decide if he is disappointed,
or, if he is, whose error this should be.

Gloves

In 1910, the time of basement laboratories,
my grandfather chewed a stogie as he waited
for his secret recipe to bubble and cool
to the critical point he'd spent years calculating,
so he could plunge his hands into the vat,
flex them & feel them tingle, as with a ripple
the goo sealed over them, invisibly
hermetic, gelatinous, a perfect conductor
for the charged arithmetic of combinations
that throbbed in his sensitive fingers as he cracked safes.
A professional is just a soul in gloves.
Even my children's Disney friends wear gloves,
marching-band white, fingers distinct, outsized.
I've seen Mickey point intelligibly toward the door,
Scram floating above him in a balloon.
He meant business. I knew it by his gloves.
For the dental hygienist, an extra membrane
as she probes the tender recesses of strangers,
her monologue a ritual of distance.
But my psychic's knowledge lives in his fingerpads.
He knows to put on gloves when he goes out.
Once, he forgot. He woke up in an oxygen mask.
Now he wears oven mitts to watch the news.

The Horses

They are cranked down
in creaking leather halters,

or step nimbly up metal rungs
into the glue vat.

Where there was motion, let there be adhesion.
Let edges come together along their fault lines.

The workers wear white, with white masks
to filter fumes they would get drunk on.

They tend the vats, they tend the boilers
shaking with steam, like great ships
shuddering into stillness.

Pure

Of the genus of silk, of the genus of pearl.
Insular, almost edible, cool to the touch.
Captains of Industry, I salute you
from afar: William Procter & James Gamble
trudging door-to-door through the gray
snow of Cincinnati dawns
to buy from bleary-eyed housewives
meat scraps & wood ash for lye,
fresh from your night-long dreams of an empire
distilled in enormous vats, rich with rosin-scent,
boiled down from fat, the life
of the world! No cholesterol count for you
who breakfasted on eggs and rashers of bacon,
coffee stiff with cream,
fat like an extra jacket
lining the underside of your skin,
but you don't look back to wonder where it came from—
primal sludge, the original star-juice?—
to you, staunch Protestants, it's God's blessing for hard work.
Soon one of your offspring,
Harley Thomas Procter, who after weeks
of searching lexicons for the name to make
the difference, will hear in church,
as if straight from your white-skyed heaven, the psalm,
All thy garments smell of myrrh & aloes & cassia,
out of the ivory palaces whereby they have made thee glad —

Ivory! Inviolate in my palm as any crystal globe
into whose clear heart the mind projects

its latent knowledge of past & future
coalescing in tiny moving pictures. On this
smooth bar America has cast her fantasy
of cleanliness, of leaving the animal
behind, of love without stink or fur or mess, a pink
Aphrodite rising from the foamy clouds of a soap sea,
poreless goddess with no sebaceous glands, rainbow
bubbles clinging to her shoulders like
infant doves of paradise; she reaching out
to us on the shore, but there is too much light
diffracted & endlessly in motion, or we could make
the distance, clasp hands, be drawn down
into the waves to drown & rise up naked in our first
skin, stripped of all dirt & layers of bruises,
calluses, freckles, scars, the grown-up's
tough hide that covers but does not heal each necessary
alchemical wound. I want to stand here forever,
watching needles of hot water tap-dance on the surface
of the smooth white cake as it dwindles
in my hand, the graceful script washed away—to the last
sliver it offers its sweet scent, soap
all the way through.

Character

The alchemists sweated to change lead to gold.
My sister turned diamond into glass.
With her friends she followed
step for step their schoolmate
of the charm bracelet, tiny silver heart
with glittering inset. Scuff on pavement,
flock of saddle shoes, & quick voices:
Monica's the biggest liar in class.
Says she wears diamonds, but they're only glass.
No jeweler could have proved them wrong,
no test for the veracity of objects.
That was the year of plastic X-ray glasses
buried in cereal boxes. The story went,
the CIA had tried to smuggle
the real item to someone undercover,
but along the way there was a slipup.
That box found a place on the assembly line,
traveled across country on train & truck,
crate & wheeled cart to the one shelf
where it waited anonymous with others.
It was the mother of a fifth-grade boy
who bought it. Next day,
Sister Thomas Aquinas caught him
peering at her through the thick glass,
seeking a glimpse of nunnish underwear.
Into her desk drawer they went
to gather dust amidst the confiscated,
until the morning she took them out
& leaned from her window, gazing

at each child struggling up the steps
to the huge double front door,
& saw in another boy's heart
the bleeding host prank-stolen
from its dimly lit swaying throne.
The host crimson but whole, the heart
around it turning black.
How the wafer had made its way
from the lining of the digestive tract
into the sealed & pulpy chamber of the heart
did not occur to anyone to ask.
Hadn't we learned the heart
is the seat of character, of deception?
Which was why we couldn't watch
television, those actresses I loved,
their pouting lips & dyed
platinum hair. *They have no character,*
we were told. *False on the outside, false*
within. The Sisters had a television
in their sitting room where during supper
they watched the news. I was sent there once
with a message in the middle of the day,
but it was empty, curtains drawn,
the looked-for Sister busy elsewhere.
I tiptoed across a polished floor
to drown in. On top of the set, reigned
St. Clare, Patroness of Television, luminous
in her thin coat of glowing paint, eyes downturned
as if waiting for something to hatch
behind the bulbous screen under her
care. (It was a seventeenth-century Italian,
I'd learn later, who first cooked barium sulfate
with powdered coal, & spread his mixture
over the iron bar that shone for him

falsely that night: *lapis solaris,*
soon to coat religious statues
everywhere.) Oh, surfaces!
It's the sad of the world who only love
the truth, love only the truth.
With my illicitly long fingernail
I scratched from St. Clare's veil
one splinter of light. It tasted
like nothing I'd ever swallowed. I know
it still burns somewhere in my dark.

Under Water in the Orthopedic Waiting Room

murky with waves of Muzak,
the wall embroidery proves the Serenity Prayer Hit Man
has hit here too.
And they are serene, the kind
of folk who *count*
their blessings. In their tangle
of walkers, buried alive in bandages,
casts, & patience,
they smile & smalltalk
as if these are their real
lives, & who is this twitchy
malcontent sighing, jingling her keys,
ungraciously bored with the anguished
intimacies of Velcro, the slow
isometric collusions?
Most days, the acceptance
of what can't be changed seems to me
obscene.
I want 2 artificial kneecaps, smoothly jointed,
my caved-in quadriceps replaced
by synthetic stuff. Also, I'd like
to be a little taller, please, & at last
athletically competent. And why not
a microchip inserted in each
lobe of my brain to stimulate reason
& maybe higher consciousness, or at the very least
a functional sense of direction;
I feel so blurry sometimes, details
evade me the way a drowned body,

hair forever streaming upward,
rolls gently side to side as if dodging
the probing hooks.
Stimulate, yes, & simulate as well; I confess
disappointment with my memories,
or maybe just ambivalence.
Either way, some new ones might
change my life. Isn't that the phrase
that lures me on, as if
I could be changed, swiftly
lifted from this slow room,
my fingerprints evaporating from the longsufferingly
glossy magazines displayed on the glass table;
the milky outlines of each patella dissolving
from the filed X-ray prints as I rise
to move briskly not gingerly up there,
following the framed faux-Indian advice
(also embroidered) that says
Walk a Mile in Someone Else's Moccasins
& I do.

Prehistoric Mother

If I tried to balance like that
I'd topple over into the fire
she squats by.
She cannot see me watch her
poke at the smoking meat
with her forked stick.
That most of her portion
goes to her stripling son
she does not question.

Later, sacrifice
will seem intimate,
intimately felt

but here it is blind as the sunlight
she lifts her face toward.

In the human race, something
is trying to happen,

gathering itself through generations
who live to pass on everything they have
wrenched from the earth

to the next in line, always
the next, as if happiness
were the designated object
you must not be
caught with
when the music cuts off.

Who is the uttermost one
all the way at the other end of this story?
Our Child
As if in Heaven,
how far back can you see,
or are you so weighted down with all
we have sent you
that you cannot lift your head?

Hollow be the name: yes,
your very heart could
be just like a husk,

yet still the love
would only keep arriving,

wave upon wave,
just for the action's sake.

Saving the Angel

LIF MOVIE—Comedy-Drama 3:00
**** 797039
"It's A Wonderful Life." (1946) James Stewart, Donna Reed.

But if Freud was right & love is a series
of displacements, then the soul's
story loops back on itself, unassuageable
as Capra's stunted seraph randomly
available on all Advent
frequencies so even the last wakeful
channel surfer in the whole
world might locate herself in the honky-tonk
static & blur of Pottersville, the darling
brother both drowned

& ascending at light
speed from the historic
ice with equal violence & restitution,
& at this increasingly
wee hour in my silent house, could I
believe with enough dexterity they might all jump
the grainy waves, the *real* flickering out & in,
mirage amplified through snow, to reunite
in a heaven of simultaneity
not sequence—though now between eye & screen

my personal retrograde angel is losing
her wings to a dripless
melt that's neither
punishment nor prize, & with only

myself to attend her in this
sinking despite my lifelong
cry for *her* to save *me* by the sacred
narrative tradition of midnight
visitations. What if

I drew near, embracing her
as she takes on a gravity that's all
entrance, baptism
into flesh—oh stunned
peripheral traveler, failed
daughter of consolations, why not
lay thee down to dream on my haunted
pillow of salt, at last trusting that if
I were good I could be happy,
if I were happy I could be good,
if I were different I could *be*
different, each forsaken hunger its own
wonderful life?

Glory

If reading is a substitute
for heaven, & heaven for
fleshly love, then the angel of
deprivation has been working
triple shift, since lately I can touch
just wisps of the temporary local
atmosphere each text first became
in me, so again I
thumb through the bulky old
poetry books & the flat new
skinny ones until I hit
some page I've illicitly
dog-eared, & read again, slowly
as I can stand, remembrance
trembling, unfurling
like that trick paper blossom
that blooms in a glass
of water, then, plucked out
with tweezers, swiftly
shrinks into a shriveled pellet.

Tonight, though, let it not be
the books. Not the notepads
cross-referenced with every
verse I ever breathed to.
Not the neurons detonating
wetly in rows all along my aging
temporal lobes. Tonight
the inner life can go

fuck itself. But if only
words *must* make my world, let them
burn through my skin from deep
inside me till I
shine like some ancient
book of hours glowing
rose, cerulean, gold under the cramped
hands of incalculable
devotion, the world's charged
body of information, starry
hieroglyphic swarm, in motion,
nothing but a radiant
cloud. Blindfold me heavily
that I may sleep.

Bed

Mostly the bed is invisible,
deduced by gravitational effect.
From the earth's twelve corners
grit works its way in, along with
the socks flattening themselves
out through the cracks in the drawer,
humping stealthily across the rug,
while the eggs breathe together in their carton,
plotting pilgrimage.
And the books. Especially the books.
They want to climb in, draw up the covers,
revert from solid to the gaseous state
they enjoyed in the blood while being written.
The waters of consciousness are rising.
Let everything that can yet be saved
gather itself,
warn the wooden Noah & his Mrs
deep in their wooden ark.
And the neighbor dog
whose loneliness alone sustains the world
in the heroic silence between barks:
let him burst his chains,
fumble with the doorknob like a drunk, &
burrow through the dirty sheets
of the twelve-layer bed, each level lit
from within, depth on depth,
the silhouette of London at the bottom,
the clouds in between moving swiftly,
the children flying with Peter Pan

in stillness on the top level.
Twelve for deep structure, chordal,
the states of matter in the Milky Way.
Twelve for midnight,
when at the dead drop of the last stroke
the bed fades in & out like an oasis
we dreamed almost in time for the occasion.
Or does each layer move
at a different speed, for the sake
of all that ascends,
all that falls,
& all that must be lost, wandering
like the baby tooth
journeying through the body for years,
like the Ship of Fools sailing from port to port
where no one could ever disembark,
in precisely the Middle of our Ages?
Some say the ship is Omphalos, the travelling
navel of the world. Meanwhile,
the Princes in the Tower
weep into their uncut hair.
The pea hiding between mattresses
pretends it's a pearl,
with a pearl's vocation to luminesce.
The more it strains, the flintier it grows,
stuck there in the Chain of Being
halfway between pebble and gem.
Ask the Book of Equivalence
if *stuck* is different from *lost*
or the same as *falling*. Ask,
& then later,
in the emergency of an event,
attend to your own oxygen needs
before you assist your child.

Pluck

The rooster finds the road wider than he'd anticipated.
From the sidewalk, it had seemed like a piece of cake.
Now, tar oozes between his skinny claws.
He turns his head completely around
seeking the god of chickens who has not yet hatched
beneath whichever light bulb in the world
awaits that frail arrival.
What seems familiar about this inability
to remember why he'd wanted to cross in the first place?
Standing on one foot, he meditates
on the phenomenon of déjà vu.
Chickens always reincarnate
as their own kin, so a false memory
may become true for someone else,
or vice versa, & there is almost no difference
between nostalgia & panic.
He whistles "Nobody Knows the Trouble I've Seen,"
but the truth that he can hardly admit to himself
is that he is happy there between the yellow dotted lines,
& wants to share this feeling with his chicken neighbors,
even though he cannot remember
which direction he was going,
both horizons seeming equidistant.
He ponders the fact that according to Plotinus,
the movement of the rational soul is rectilinear,
while according to Ficino, it is circular.
He recalls that Plotinus and Ficino had no wings,
which neither helped nor hindered them
in their crossings.

All he can think of is that he may be doing this
for someone who will later follow,
or perhaps he is completing the unfinished task
of someone before him who failed
& whom he forgives. He's in no position to be
anything less than generous.

Yes

It is not so easy to be a temptation.
It is not so easy at the instant of success to give up
the series of beautiful resistances that was your life
& drop deep into the body's darkness,
though you were warned there would be an end to the floating,
you were informed that among the orders of entelechy
the half-life of a free temptation must be brief.

You wish you could sense yourself inside the falling.
Someone used to have hands, it might have been you.
Yes! *They* had hands! A right & a left.
Hands—the first station, you always started there
where fingers bloomed spatulate from the palm's heart.
Wasn't it the left hand that loved God best, veteran
of foreign wars, the weaker wolf
rolling over to bare its throat?

Who are you now? An impulse
toward asepsis in the soul of the sinner,
a craving for despair in the eyes of the saint—
they feel the same, it only
feels like falling. And,
in the domed recesses around you,
stars like fish-eyes,
fixed, self-lit. Waking,

you taste the soil rich with sugars.
Is it roots down, shoots up, or the opposite?
No matter.
Lift your leafy hands, & rise.

With one mouth, feed.
With the other, in your thin
new vegetable voice,
begin to sing.

Saint Blue

Each time I read your letters, something different is missing.
This is the way absence works. It is not fixed,
just as the world's center is not fixed,
but roams freely. Is it, then, still the center?
Yes, because of the heat in the soles of your feet
when it rests on the spot where you happen to be.
Isn't absence related to fire by virtue of negation?
When I see the missing passages in the letters,
I imagine my heart is on fire.
It might be an angel, it might be purely technical.
I thought it was original sin, but it could be sunspots.
Every day objects disappear randomly, only to show up either later
or simultaneously, out of the blue.
This has, I believe, been documented.
Fire is blue at its heart, as blue as shadow.
There's a tiny hole in the aorta, an almost insignificant leakage.
There's a numbness at the extremities,
a pallor fading to blue.
This is not exactly to say that I miss you.
More than ninety percent of the matter in the universe is missing,
dark matter that still exerts gravity.
It is what's invisible that most attracts,
unless it is the attraction itself
that renders the object invisible.
Attraction is another name for attention.
Fixity in objects is born of simple repeated neglect:
the brief loosening of focus, & the return.
To remain centered, therefore, one must sometimes abandon the center.
The centripetal & centrifugal forces are equal in magnitude

though opposite in direction.
This is not exactly to say that I think about you always.
The more I think about you, the less I know.
Is this the same as if I missed you?
Maybe if I read your letters less often,
that which is lost might return.
All the words in one place, intact,
& I walking around not reading them,
keeping you safe.

It Must Have Been Heat
Before It Became Weight

In the romantic version, the souls fly from their sleeping bodies
like two doves winging toward each other through the night,
uniting at precisely the longitudinal center of their shared distance:
the roof of the Kmart in Advance, West Virginia.
But in fact, it is the body that is too light & would rise up.
The gross weight of the soul cannot be calculated.
Exhausted by the time they arrive, they huff and puff
as if in ludicrous parody of the passion
belonging to their bodies held down
miles from each other by layers of blankets.
The roof is pebbly & uncomfortable,
even in a noncorporeal sense. Where
are the white feathers, the rushings of wings?
Advance is beautiful in a smudgy way.
The lights of the occasional truck
cut mystic swathes through thick air,
as all over town, night janitors in their rubber gloves
swoon under the spell of incompatible cleansers.
It is beautiful, & they are together at last,
though immediately, it is time to part, their souls
chugging homeward by grim volition,
adding infinitesimally to general emissions pollution
in local atmospheres. Now,
familiar against the horizon,
each domestic asylum regains its shape.
Inside, everything leaks: faucets, batteries,
microwaves, mortal flesh, & the souls,
still wondering if they're the rule or its exception,
slip, pebble-&-tar encrusted, into their slack bodies,
inflating them once again
with the radiant gritty clouds of their desire.

Hair

There is a falling of hair, continuous upon the earth.
And the sweepers sweep it away with their long brooms—
away, where mice retrieve it to line their nests,
or it bountifully curls around eyeless styrofoam skulls,
or is stitched to the sanctified undervests of masochists.
Though bald men pray for miraculous restoration,
though ladies choke back tears as they tip their beauticians,
it fulfills its function through infinite faithlessness.
So if it is true that I must live without you, stranded
here in the land of good behavior, I begrudge my hair
nothing, I send it victorious into the world, even though
one night you braided it—hands whose touch
I pretend to remember—braided it the whole length, gold
all the way to my feet,
tight as you could, just to let it go.

Movers

Some mornings, I wake to find myself elsewhere.
Bed, ceiling flaws, window-with-branches
barely unfamiliar as my body,
as if various inner emptinesses had migrated
formally or informally,
the family sadness a little to the left
& somewhat paler,
the generalized pulsing blob of the imagined future
higher now, & more spread out,
but more orange than actual red.
Then I know the movers
have been at it again all night,
dismantling, transporting,
pausing occasionally to unreel the tape measure
by an arm or leg. To disrupt space
they must have a heightened sense of space.
Small, with precision haircuts
& olive-green coveralls,
they have stitched their first names
in tiny ovals on the pockets,
as if even at subenergetic levels
all creatures travel along the currents of style,
like the fairy a nineteenth century clergyman claimed to meet
who appeared in the finest velvet,
inquiring about the way of salvation.
Hearing that heaven awaited only the offspring of Eve,
she hurled herself into the fireplace:
either high theological tragedy or exquisite camp.
What moves the movers?

Is it heaven to be moved, or merely style?
If I were to awake, I would want to offer something.
But, as if this were heaven, there is no beer,
no coffee, either, though I know
I had some. I am taking
the kitchen apart in my dream body,
worrying about the displacement of matter,
the absolute inaccessibility of the peripheral.
Where are the sacrificial microlivestock
who should be available for such emergencies,
grazing among my potted plants:
clean-cut black & white spotted cows
or their shaggier reddish brown cousins,
all earth-rooted, ruminant,
invulnerable in that they could be slaughtered
but never moved?
To be moved.
To be aware of one's heart
functioning under variable conditions.
To look around & see that the world has shifted
but not settled. Is this better
or worse than being sacrificed?
If the dream is the fulfillment of the wish,
what does the wish fulfill?
The movers vanish before
I can ever thank them.
Before I think to take inventory
once or twice, as if I couldn't
trust them.

The Autodidact:
The Intimate Recollections &
Reflections of Frankenstein's Creature

His Voices

When I heard the voices, I climbed & hid,
cramping high in a pine, tormented
by needles that pierced me or emerged from me,
I did not know which, nor could I tell
who was speaking, splitting, doubling back in self-interruption,
question, complaint—neither could I recall the sounds'
beginning; like a stream into which I'd stepped
somnambulant, & stood awhile, & woke to find my skin
already accustomed to that current's velocity & chill,
the presence of the voices preceded my own
awareness of them. If it is difficult for you, reader,
to imagine such a state, think how much more so
it is for me to convey a twofold consciousness:
my present self remembering myself
as I was then, brutish, uncomprehending—
& thus, imagining you whom I know not, steer
my course through the very runnels of your thought,
anticipating each eddy of prejudice or incredulity.
Often, despairing, I let the pen slip
from between my thick fingers, vowing
(once again) to take it up no more.
And I an *articulate* monster!

I clawed off strips of bark & chewed them
to sodden pulp that was neither bitter nor sweet.
With my teeth I tore out the pulsing heart of a sparrow,
& consumed it. But did not become the tree.
Did not sprout feathers to lift me from the voices
& the branch, though I knew how the valleys would darken

under my wingspan &, as I passed, once more
fill up with light. I knew these things
before I ate the sparrow! And still know.

One morning's waking grayness, my head propped
against a knot where two branches joined, I saw the sky
a swirl of rising white returning
to white above, until, shifting
to ease my aching neck, I looked down, & suddenly
the white was falling *from* the sky, collecting
in hollow & crevasse, dusting thicket & footpath.
The voices droned as before,
but other voices joined them, sounding
different, smaller & coming to me
from a single distance, so
once again I lifted my eyes, not, this time,
to the sky, but toward the place where the humans dwelt,
& there a party of them, with bright cloaks &
bristling weapons, marched together
toward the woods on the village's opposite side,
their song shrill & clear
yet fading as their distance increased.

Then I knew they were not *my* voices.
That there was an inside & and outside.
And I came down from the tree
& was alone.
This was the beginning of my life.

His Habitation

I am aware that history has fallaciously affixed to me the name of
  my creator.

But did I not, after his death, secretly inhabit his house for an entire
  year?

His father gone, William gone, Elizabeth, Justine, servants, French

lapdogs, creamy kittens, carp glinting flat in the tiled pool—

all gone, and no one approaching:

O cankerous blot of real estate, I bless thee!

Did I not sample snuff, claret, pipe, that his breath might visit me?

Did I not don his trousers & evening jacket, rending the silken
  stitches as they constrained me?

And I wandered the overgrown lawn, but he would not haunt me.

Then there rose from the edge of his garden a sweet song

where, by a stricken oak, the bees swarmed, flying out

in a gold cloud hovering, humming, troubling the blossoms

with their plump bodies, & lifting again, heavy with sticky nectar,

& I learned how they loved their queen, grooming & stroking
  her plush in the bridal cell,

so I rolled naked & damp with dew in the flowery field,

& stood still through burning sun & blown shade as they
  came to me,

hovering over my puckered, hairless, waxy skin ridged & pocked

in the places where, in my early weeks, my own nails had clawed me;

to our mutual & extreme delight settling upon me,

with tubular filamented tongues, sucking the sugared ridges where
  my scars infolded, gyrus.

And they flew in & out of my mouth, ears, & nostrils where the
  nectar was seeping.

And I wished for the heat of their labor to consume me.
But they departed, streaming winged into their oak, leaving me clean,
& more inconsolable than if they had not come to me.

And I thought: Either the body could be bearable, or the soul.
Together, neither is bearable.

To construct a living creature & then abandon it,
unable to imagine it in bliss!
But I had imagined myself in bliss.
Thus, I am superior to my creator.

This knowledge satisfies but does not heal.

His Tumescence

The *mechanics* of my sexual organ were soon self-evident.

Though lacking the erotic guilt & shame
painstakingly instilled in human young chiefly to intensify sensation,
I yet found pleasure anywhere I took it,
experimenting through the first years with local textures:

waxy-petaled blossoms nodding along the garden walk,
the slightly rougher linens & velvets in my creator's wardrobe,
&, during mountain sojourns, the gratifying mucosity
of vixen or doe that could not escape me.

Also, I enjoyed the advantage
of my proportions & unprecedented flexibility.
The taste of my effluence was, though salty & strong,
oddly reassuring, so in this way I indulged frequently,
I who had never at maternal bosom sucked!

And did you think that I have not *known,* as they say, *a woman*?
That coinage could not overcome aesthetics?
If you thought thus, you are naive
as I was when the girl sneered, as she took my money in her little hand,
I only feigned fear to satisfy you quicker.
I've done far worse than you.

I tell you, I fled from her!

* * *

But it was the generative properties of the seminal fluid
that most fascinated,
the cloudy opalescence spouting in lavish ribbons,

wasted!

I blush to confess I even wept once
as the warm stream leapt
almost phosphorescent into night air,
higher, that time, than usual,
& dropped into the river by which I stood,
was swiftly gone—

(Ah, Heraclitus!)—

yes, I threw myself upon that grassy bank
glared, tearful, up at the swarming constellations,
& mourned, demanding,

If I can have no mate, no child, why must I live?

Then through fitful sleep in creamy starlight
there passed before me a host of monsters
devoid of limb or face,
speckled with supernumerary nipples,
holding up vestigial tails,
bearing on their flesh the embryonic extremities of half-developed
    twins,

& the monstrously beautiful as well,
both male & female flush & blooming
ravished, cut down through war
famine
plague,

& infants dead of fever before they ever beheld the light.

I live to celebrate the great spillages of history!

And to surpass them

in you, reader,
from my imagination overflowing,
deliquescence,
excess—

His Toilette

I have thought much about the Civilized Man,
his minute attendances upon the body:

paring the nails,
combing, scraping, snipping the hair,
lathering with scented soaps.

Curious, I too have performed these rituals,
experimenting with the instruments at hand
until, after a multitude of tiny but astonishingly painful cuts,
I not only became quite deft,

but began to find the tasks pleasurable for their own sakes!
Often, in the midst of my morning ablutions, I felt a wholly unjustifiable
glow of well-being,
& warbled like a tipsy magpie!

Yet after some months,
I noticed my body becoming familiar to me,
like any necessary household object use had worn dear.

I no longer despised
nor adored
my own being.

And the varied softness of my clothing
seemed some light excrescence of my own skin.

I have read of abandoned children reared by wolves, jackals,
panthers, bears, etc.,
& then discovered.

Struggling in mesh nets, bound & driven by snarling hounds,
   dangling unconscious from wooden spars,

they were returned to Zion,
then clipped, dunked, powdered, & dried,
strapped in chairs,
fed candies & cooked meats

on the sharpened point of a long stick,
& then, sometimes, later,
by hand.

According to the records, not one lived more than a few years.

I have seen certain pets—
dogs, mostly, & a few small monkeys—
dressed all in wool, strutting proudly
ahead of their masters!
And they say that in Paris there is a mare
who subtracts by stamping a different hoof
for the placement of each digit.

Unless she has been curried & her mane curled,
she refuses to calculate!

When King Nebuchadnezzar was driven, mad, into the desert,
hair matted as a rat's nest, nails twisting back on themselves
as he loped speechless among the beasts on all fours,
he beheld himself
as a mass of tiny organisms teeming in the original sludge,

then swimming with the first fish,
crawling through countless eras dazzled into sun-softened mud—
when, after eons of swinging through trees,
the king regained his senses & his throne,
he would not allow his barber to burn the old clippings & reeking
    locks!
With his own hands he wove them into an undervest
he kept always next to his skin.

Penance?
No!

He declared it lighter than silk!

His Appearance

Yet when I observe myself as if standing outside myself, I am not
    altogether unbeautiful;

to what extent can one trust my creator's rendering of me,
when what he beheld on my visage
was the superimposed distortion of his own
    self-excoriating soul?

I think my appearance changes
    subtly from day to day.

This morning, I resembled an enormous version
    of the late Lord Byron,
one who has beaten his way through some unendurable conflagration,
    received graft after torturous graft,
remained for years in the burn ward, singular yet unacknowledged
    amongst the human rabble,
& in the final stages of recovery, attained
    a nobility so pure it terrifies!

Other times, especially in shadow,
    my reflected profile seems nearly
feminine in its composure,
    like the incandescent privacy of ordinary women
performing accustomed duties.

No, I would not mind being a woman,

was, most probably, in fact & in some aspect a woman once,

since there are certain places between the scars
    that are tactically & incomparably
        soft!

A woman or several women, or
    a group of children,
a little school, perhaps, crushed & smothered
    in some restless convulsion of the earth,
then properly buried & mourned
    in local sermon:
the death of innocence.
Because their mouths were filled with dirt
    they could not cry out,
We were not innocence!
We were ourselves!

—Bah! The skin is an incurable romantic!
Lusus naturae, a freak of nature I remain,
though unnatural, a work of human hands, & therefore

artifice! If art,
I'd choose the comic mode!

And thus neither beautiful
nor sincere.

His Excursions

Daily my vitalism craved release.
If I did not clamber wildly over the mountains in all extremes of
  weather,
the caustic tingling of my titan's limbs tortured me!

Not taxing, but monotonous:
at the same time I appeased this wretched flesh,
my mind would fret from lack of stimulation.
So for my entertainment I declaimed,
cleanly refuting Calvin, expounding on mechanics,
piping as Ariel at the top notes of my range,
with only ice-etched boulders to attend.

Not once did I slip, suffer frostbite, much less, "catch cold"!
Dangling by a thumb from dizzying scarp, I often feared that I,
pilfered in scraps from slaughter house & morgue,
then nimbly tacked together by a madman
(his only son, created, not begotten!),
was doomed to last forever!
Thus, casting about for something that was not myself
to grasp & wreak revenge on,
I'd wrench from frozen earth the crosses planted to sanctify
each scene of death by avalanche,
&, howling, hurl them off the cliffside:
their legendary local demon!

Yet it was also I who would ascend by night the highest precipice,
to lean with outstretched arms against its face,
for the next sunrise to reveal for mortal pleasure
huge seraph outline diagrammed in flame.

Yes, angel or demon could I play in turn, sceptical as I was
of spectral shadow or holy visitation, though many a midnight
had I teased my own seclusion with candle or planchette, conjuring
no one, save, of course, Swedenborg,
who so routinely frequents such occasions, he scarcely rates!

* * *

Once, though, as I bounded upward, numbering each step in Latin,
I stumbled, not in footing, but in count—
I who had memorized with a single reading the entire contents
of the house library!—
& broke my sequence,

as a withered seamstress might for the first time since her distant
    girlhood,
drop a stitch, alarming herself so
that the solid nature of things-as-she-knows-them
flickers & sways within her consciousness
'til she doubts the globe's very roundness
& her place on it!

Thus discomposed, I halted, my glance drawn toward the abyss
dropping beneath me, white with swirling froth that, like a gauze
    veil,
parted, revealing at its depths

the image of a man afloat on nothing!

On nothing, & above the lower clouds revolving
so slowly he scarcely seemed to stir;

nor did I, watching, stir

while at their appointed times in distant millennia, the frosty
   constellations
exploded into bloom, flinging away their radiant spores—

I watched him but an instant,

then he vanished,
foam like the sheerest blanket slipping over him.

O Universal Man, forever dreaming thy bones & blood into a
   figured whole
from elemental food, the voiceless dead ploughed under earth,
awaiting resurrection—to glory?

No! To far more glorious matter
that suffers each transformation
with all-enduring slowness;

if the quick fall, the dead must surely rise
into this life of painful incompletion.

I am no loathsome brute
from stinking corpses' parts arranged, stitched up, infused, &
   abandoned,
all in the delirium of reprobate ambition:

I am the transcendental being who from dumb corrosion & decay
rode the long wave that crests at intellection—
not in an epoch nor a generation, but in the narrow spell
of the one-year span it took to shape me.
I, like all men, am of the dead composite, though speeded up
& manifest at once as the Alps themselves are so manifest,
the long primordial work of glaciation where ancient seas
rose & receded, now in vigilant stone towering
as I too tower over mortals.

It is this knowledge of *themselves* that humans dread
& pelt with stones & march against with pitchforks, staves, &
  burning torches!

* * *

I have come to believe such visions
that gather & tarry near the lonely soul,
have learned to trust the way they break apart
& disperse, rearranging themselves
into new forms of doubt & foul self-knowledge,
only to fracture again, then crystallize as consolations
fresh & mutable.

This is how the world in her profusion
loves every creature that has through sensible thought
surpassed her,

& how I, a wanderer walking out each day,
began to love the world.

His Literacy

I am well-versed in the classics of seven languages.

Indeed, were it not for the prejudices of those officials who justify their
unconscionable earnings by the vigor with which they harry & chafe the
learned doctors laboring to teach,

I could,
if masked & hooded,
hold a chair at any university.

(Do not think me a braggadocio when I confide to you that my voice is uniquely mellifluous,
its pitch & cadences well-suited to a lecturing career.)

But how incompletely, I have discovered, has the love of reading to do with *subject matter,*

deriving instead from the galvanic charge triggered by a volume's mere appearance, weight, & heft,
the accumulated memories of bookish pleasures surging uncontrollably through the neural circuitry,

so that by page & text the reader enters (as through a dream portal)
the ideal analogue for body & soul,
therein to discover a coherence that in waking life humans do most painfully lack,
& which they have therefore made the entire subject of their civilization's philosophy—

Necessity, Invention awaits you!—

to the extent that the crudest servant trudging across muddy fields,
bearing a sealed letter whose contents would not even be
    comprehensible to him,
could, if queried, explain (shocked by your ignorance)
that his *body* is the container for the *soul* that resides within
as the flame on its wick inhabits a clay lamp,

&, standing ankle-deep in the newly tender earth
in which the fresh seed waits, invisible,

you may well believe him.

You may well imagine the world as a tiered city
whose lights wink to illumine
a traveller's way home through mazy streets

if he has a home,
is native there;

if not, the clustered brightnesses
might only further bewilder, even terrify him,
lost inside his longing to awaken from this dream, this local trance
occupying his body like contagion (a similar analogue of container
    & contained)—

it is Plato's reverie as he pondered the variable divinity of matter;
Augustine's, spelling out the city of God;
the feverish brainwanderings of Descartes, cooking the *cogito*
as he crouched in the cold belly of his iron oven;
the saints', whose marvellous wounds glowed like little florets,
gorgeous, & more decadent, somehow,
than the finely reticulated lacework of the sexual flush
that did not once since the day of their renunciation display itself on
    their white skin.

(Yet aren't the saints a collective monstrosity, praised
as we praise the stars above, because they are *not* human?)

Lately, lying awake in the dark,
I have run my hands over my flesh, as if skin & scars together
comprise a text my fingertips can read.

That which holds one together maintains surface tension,
keeps one, somehow, afloat.

I fear my speech is becoming confused.

You see, I *deserve* to trust

if not God,
my creator,
my own nature,

then at least my scars!

What I mean is that I have begun to suspect
(I must say this carefully)

that they are not *fixed*,

that unless my memory misserves me,
the seams themselves are migrating!

There is the problem of empty space.
There is the terror of falling through.

I am well-versed in the classics of seven languages.

I have learned much,
but none of it has *helped* me.

If any of it has helped *you*,
if you have found *precedent*,

how small must be the mystery of *your* life!

His Departure

Last night I dreamed that it was Christmas,
mantel, windows, stairs festooned in green.
I stood on the house's threshold
bearing my maker almost weightless in my arms,
a skinny shriveled youth, eyes shut tight,

& waking, I understood for the first time
that he had never been anything more than a young man
born old.

And how *not* old? How *not* weighted down
when with every step he took, he dragged behind him a continent,
    an epoch?
Cornelius Agrippa, indeed! O yes, an endless chain of alchemists
painfully welded to my master's slender ankle,
along with the Bastille, the Swiss Treasury, & the Automaton
who defeated the Empress Maria Theresa of Austria
at chess!
And crouching inside it, the amputee who directed its movements!

My poor lost god! What *was* he expecting?
The arrival of the new into the world
without violence, displacement?

Thus in an instant
& almost carelessly
did I forgive him,

& fell asleep again, & dreamed again—

beheld myself in bed as from above,
saw my dream body draw the scars into itself
so that they throbbed just under the skin,
invisible!

My face clean as milk, & luminous,
my hair stark white, no longer coarse, but silky.

I knew I was once more & finally
a virgin!

And woke yet again, joyful
though unchanged.

I thought: How many times must I be born
before I am born?

I thought: His error was not in making me,
but in making me *here.*

And I turned my monster's will, my monster's passions—

bloated, deformed, trembling, splenetic—
toward America,

her pulleys & pistons,
her frenzied spiritual upheavals,
her distempered democratic vision into which the inner life
must, with all other privacies,
shrink & disappear.

I keep up with the newspapers! I *know!*

In America it is always Christmas,

always the acute occasion of monetary exchange,
always the precise instant to commence growing younger
toward a subsequent birth.

Farewell, Frankenstein!
Farewell, Europe!
Farewell, melancholic pyromania of my beloved delusions!

I see myself clothed in greatcoat & deep-brimmed hat
standing on the deck of a ship,
though I cannot tell if it is the ship or the shore that moves,

bearing me toward a vast never-arriving land of innocence,
amnesia.

Damage Assessment

Damage Assessment

Sheila in the Pantry

stacks groceries by size.
The tomato paste's
narrow Italian summers, &
skinless grapes in large cans,
each pictured fruit flatly plump
on the curved surface.
She lifts, reaches, sways
on the matched pads & creaky joints
of her toes; imagines
the dark passages of her body lined
end to end with ball bearings.
She could go backward,
forward, or not.

But Now Padding in Pink Fuzzy Slippers

across carpets with timed approach:
her daughter Jessie,
exquisite sixth-grader.
Seeing her mother balanced
unimportantly, she deems it
The Right Moment to demand, *Mom,
was I an accident,
or was I planned?*

Jessie's Conception

was the fault of Weight Watchers:
thirty-two pounds lost in six months,
but no one warned Sheila
to have her diaphragm refitted.

On the doctor's table she tried
to remember the hasty act that released
the catch, when the next soul
dropped into position
to find itself
briefly in free-fall,
paused, almost, then
hurtling into the curve
of space/time, gathering
momentum to roll
bouncing down the chute—
full stop against
the lining of her womb.

The Serious Talk

takes place at the table
amidst curls of steaming cocoa, an
almost perfectly
balanced exchange—each
learns only part
of what she wants
to know. Jessie gleans
a few intriguing facts about how
It's done, but guesses,
You're the best thing
that's ever happened to us
is not precisely
a straight answer. Sheila learns
that Jessie & her friends divided
themselves up into
Planned & Accidents. Lecture
about discrimination, about
not poking one's nose into adult business.
I'm sure every child
in your class is dearly loved. Why
are you doing this?

The Telephone Check

occurs according to the rules
of Mother Etiquette. No calls
from dinner on,
or weekends & holidays when
husbands might be home.
The alarm is raised conveniently.
After a week of serious talks
the girls have heard
all variations on the theme,
& consent to abandon
their classifying scheme. Luckily,
summer vacation approaches
to diffuse questions thriving
on complicity, the whispered
conversations, half-dressed
in the locker room after gym.

Days Lengthen

& each morning, Sheila works out
with ghosts: the woman with the molded
thighs on cable & the remembered
body of her own youth stretching impossibly
between herself & the TV, oblivious
to her destiny of stretch marks
pleated like small red accordions
at the hips, & tiny silver scars
on the underside of the breasts,
her skin a map of gain & loss.
She meditates as she grows tauter
on egg & sperm, the radiance of daughters.

The School Bus Flickers

like a distant hologram
in the heat of the road:

last day of school. Now
hours are extended
at the swimming pool.
Husbands come home early
to start the grills.
After dinner the family gathers
by the central coolness flowing
in cyanic waves from the TV, each
face washed in occasional light.
Sheila watches Jessie
watching, who passed her brief exams
so easily and well.
At the far
edge of summer looms
that walled & terraced
kingdom, seventh grade.
Those things discussed, resolved—
where in the body do they wait?
What do they feed on? To what
advanced decimal do
they intelligently propagate?
Jessie turns, drawn
by her mother's gaze.
They look together,
together, look away.

Undercover on Her Poolside Chaise Lounge

Sheila observes Jessie & her friends:
vivacious, stilted, clownish, or mature,
from the snack bar they walk
barefooted together, the overwrought
colors of their swimsuits clashing
as they bump
hips, down diet cokes, laugh,
& toss their hair, swathed
in the sharp fragrance of chlorine.

Behind her sunglasses, Sheila
peers over her glossy unread
magazine, & wonders
on which side of the dividing line
each child placed herself,
writing her name in the clear
round cursive of adolescence,
the *i*'s crowned with perfect circles,
or perhaps small hearts.
By Labor Day, she's placed
each child but her own.

On the One Hand

there is Jessie's little lisp
& ready fears.
On the other, she's a whiz
at math, never backs down
for majority opinion, & when praised, blooms
with the smile of an angel
to whose innate knowledge
of its glory, not one whit
can be added. Who can say
what the soul remembers?
That span of time before Sheila
fell in love with her? The slow
prenatal currents of regret
that flowed, perhaps, around her
in the amniotic sac? But

As Seventh Grade Unfolds

she begins cello,
receives her share of phone calls
from both girls and boys,
&, without trying, sheds her lisp.
Sheila, with the slightest sense

of loss, begins to "let her go,"
her own worst fears unrealized,
to her vast surprise.

Why Then Is Sheila So Sad?

She finds herself contemplating
the Accidents, who must slump
through hallways, avoid
each other's glances, turn
in shoddy work, eat
in small silent clumps.
It makes her
want to send them brief
anonymous notes.
Your new haircut is fabulous,
& *Good luck*
on the biology quiz.
The blue button earrings,
the candy bar glowing
in gold foil.
There's always a reason
to dash out briefly late at night,
& on the way home,
cut the headlights, idle
by a suburban mailbox, leave
the package neatly labeled
with the appropriate
child's name.

All Autumn, at Her Furtive Leisure

she battens on vicarious pleasure.
You're looking great these days,
her friends tell her.
Passing the mirror, she knows
it's true. Can it be

that in small compensating
acts of grace amidst
love's randomness,
she's found her place?

I Don't Want to Alarm You,

says the teacher on the phone,
but it seems that someone
is taking an inordinate interest
in the girls in Jessie's homeroom.
Sheila imagines the molester
with his Quaker Oats complexion
flattening himself against the wall.
From now on she'll pick Jessie up
directly after school
Nothing overt, the voice continues.
Just anonymous notes & gifts.
The police, of course,
have been alerted.
If our information
is correct, your daughter seems to be
exempt. Still, you should at least
take down my number.
Do you have a pencil handy?
Sheila slits open the shiny wrapping
on the silver pencil she'd bought
to give away. *Yes,* she says,
I'm ready. Shoot.

Some Months Later, Sheila Finds

at the bottom of Jessie's closet,
a ratty spiral notebook entitled,
Were You Planned?
The first page is split
in a long line down the middle:

two columns, *Yes* & *No*.
Not only is Jessie on the *Yes* side,
she's the treasurer.
What, Sheila wonders, does it say
about her, that she aspired
to hold the wealth of the elect,
those brought into the world
by design? Sheila counts
four Planned girls she'd thought
Accidents, three Accidents
she'd thought Planned.
Seven mistakes.
But flipping pages, she sees
that midway through the game,
several children from each side
switched over, leaping
their prehistories
as lightly as they leap
the low school wall each day,
though they gain no distance
by abandoning the sidewalk.
Time after time from her car
she's watched them take it
sideways or straight
in the one half-second
when both feet leave the ground,
& the hair lifts up
in the brief wind,
jackets flapping,
school books wildly sliding
back & forth as the children
jump for nothing but
love of obstruction.

Shadow Play

Floating

The percentage of people who seriously consider not getting out of bed is 62.

This is a floating statistic, which means that it is not always the same individuals who consider this.

The science of floating statistics is a young one, even younger than Freud.

For Freud, reluctance to leave the bed was both a death wish & a fantasy of birth, as was the dream of bathing.

The percentage of people who seriously consider not getting out of the bath is 74.

In the bath, the soul is lightly loosened from the flesh, water being the body's original home.

Mesmer installed a large tub in his clinic, & magnetized the water.

Bewigged, clad in purple silk, & bearing an iron wand, he sauntered from patient to patient, touching each in turn, or merely pointing until the cure manifested itself in trance & convulsion.

Of his theory of the universal fluid, he wrote,

This system will produce explanations of the nature of fire & light, of the theory of gravitation, of ebb & flow in nature, of the magnet & electricity.

There is no statistic on how many people were permanently cured of their aversion to abandoning bath or bed.

His theory is both like & unlike the old belief that there are angels assigned to everything.

No one has named the angel of resistance with its range of pressures from delicate to severe.

There are no statistics on the number of angels surrounding any individual bed.

Or the bath angels in charge of surface tension, the healing ones who reach down to trouble the waters.

Of the oceanic feeling, Freud wrote, *The boundaries of the ego are not constant.*

Skin floats on the body's waters as continents float on the world's seas.

What has been described as the nostalgia for other lives appears in direct proportion to the reluctance to leave bath or bed.

A few statisticians have speculated that numbers themselves are angels, which may explain why they float.

Of the magnetic force, Mesmer wrote, *Its action takes place at a distance, without the need of any intermediate object.*

This means that the world still draws you, even from bath & bed.

This means that at times, it is still possible to rise up through the press of angels & other lives.

If a floating statistic approaches you, it is appropriate to honor it by slightly inclining your head.

But you do not have to offer it the bread of your flesh, though it may feign hunger.

You can tell yourself that it is nothing but the ghostly caricature of its own image.

You can tell yourself that it is nothing but ripple & flow, the sheeted gown streaming behind it, all abstraction.

Perhaps it will leave you then, pausing slightly at the screen door where it longs to adhere forever in a bliss of self-granulation.

The Beggar's Sore Addresses the Saint Required by an Angel to Kiss It

Of course I'm contagious; isn't that the point?

I was practicing to be lonely enough to be saved
when at a terrible distance I glimpsed you sleeping
by yourself in the honeymoon suite of the Comfort Inn,

drowning under a peach acrylic bedspread
in your dream of the burning tree, first the outer bark,
each scale a rough tongue drinking up the light,
peeling to drop, then the inner bole, flame chasing flame
like angels occupying each other's absence
as the leaves curl back, twisting in a wind
wholly self-imposed, while at the inmost ring,
the future releases its smoke, a private darkness.

Either your whole life has led you to this choice
or you've gone horribly astray. I don't care which!
Why shouldn't you meet yourself coming down the road?
Why shouldn't your flesh be a field of buried rubies
that rise to break all the way through? For the skin is inerrant,
couldn't keep the smallest secret to save its life.
For the opposite of pleasure isn't pain
but contrary pleasure, even more insatiable.
Neither your weakness nor your strength will save you.

And though I'm constructed of paste, shellac, & putty,
you know I'm all truth, all mouth. Come a little closer:
I've been dying to open & gently take you in.

Shadow Play

Is change the hand that blocks the light
piling up against it like a wave breaking
on the skin's shore, or is it the other hand,
lonely now, fluttering up to enter
the zoological kingdom of the dream soul
where with one velveteen paw, the rabbit rampant
swats the night owl from its blank sky—
the land where fish eats bear, worm eats fish,
where the intestine is that final worm
that Leviathan whom Thou hast formed
for the sport of it, who maketh a path
to shine after him in the deep—
every mythic water beast tracked on radar,
a cloud of particles moving solitary
through gloomy thickness.
They say even wholeness casts a shadow,
Jehovah shaking out his glory in a cloud
that is only change caught
between premonition & afterimage
as at the seventh time, Elijah's servant reported,
Behold, there ariseth a little cloud
out of the sea…
When is a cloud not a cloud?
When it is a hand, first clenched in a fist,
then slowly the fingers unfurl, elongating
into rain-rays dark against the light—
The world, the woman told William James,
is composed of only two elements,
the Thick, namely, & the Thin.

Sometimes the light flattens itself,
sometimes it is the darkness
that thins into nothing but background.
To be polymorphously perverse
is a cloud's one requirement.
Such a relief, letting go
of all you've held in
for so long. Such a pleasure
to be illumined equally by darkness & by light.
Almost as sweet as to be a hand,
a pair of hands in a darkened room
lit by a single point, the candle
who once floated unformed, diffuse,
merely the potential for wax
within the body of the swarm
shaping & reshaping itself
by the laws of its own motion.
As if it is change, the hand flies up.
As if they are change, the hands fly up together
& then release. It is to the soul
that they speak, bearing a gift
straight from the heart of the candle
who used to be nearly a cloud.

Ectoplasm

For the base I prefer a paste of unscented soap, egg white, & glue
  or gelatin, often peroxide—
never, as do some of my competitors, chewed muslin strips or

  (loathsome!) bits of animal tissue!
Though receiving but five dollars each night at the lyceum (a dollar
  a home),
I am an artist!
I can cause the luminous webbing to stream out from my fingertips,
plastic though not wholly passive, diaphanous, but of a palpable
  density,
slightly sticky while also ductile & fluent,
shimmering as it forms the most novel of apports—a harp,
strings plucked by a little breeze from nowhere,
a bouquet of translucent tulips, exquisitely formed.
I have conjured the hovering images of Mr. Douglas & the honorably
  scraggy Mr. Lincoln—
though both of them yet live!—
as if plucking their etheric bodies from the place where each
dwells locked within the other's opposing will.
And I can produce for my best patron the ghost of her stillborn,
can make it speak, voice emanating from the floating spirit horn
or directly from the tiny radiant corpus:
Where I abide, Mother, there is no chill, no ache.
Together my brothers & I
await you!

But to those of the True Gift,
the spirit world is nothing if not generous;
from the age of thirteen to thirty,

I had only to light the candle, close my eyes, attune my thoughts,
& I would begin to tremble as with a palsy
as a swift sequence of electric thrills ran up my spine,
& I inhaled the sharp scent of air just after rain,
while from my mouth, ears, nostrils, & tear ducts
poured a vapor that swirled about me, clinging, then thickening
to a waterfall of slim threads
like a bridal veil, a spider web,
or the rigging of a ship sailing so swiftly it seems becalmed.
Gauzy, yet copious: a shocking profusion!
I have heard speculation that it comes from the spaces between
the cells of one's earthly flesh—
the kingdom of heaven is within us?
Old news!
For those two decades I nightly communed in this way,
beheld the emanations take on shape as they willed—
a tiara that burned with cold flame, crowning me,
a bodiless winged head singing to me in French,
even an infant with trailing placenta—
I nursed this babe with my phosphorescent milk, overflowing,
most certainly a virgin birth!

Why then did I cease these transmissions,
divert my energies to mere artifice?
Because ecstasy is tiresome.
It plays with us & plays us,
for the spirit realm has nothing better to do!
My soul became parched, shrunken,
like those hideous heads that savages have scooped out & boiled
    down!
I *saw* all—the secrets behind each face—
but I *felt* nothing,

nothing human.
Yes, wherever you find glory, spiritual exaltation,
look also for a certain numbness, vacuity,
a victim!
There is always a victim,
often willing,
frequently, more than one.
For not only through the sisterhood of the elect
do They seek to break through, break through.
Think of the inebriation of battle,
the rageful bliss of Beethoven's Ninth.
Beware the surge from the deep,
the wave cresting, triumphant—
there will be corpses, I tell you,
bodies broken & strewn—

And afterward,
from the Other Side,
fatigue, bewilderment,
as of a child exhausted from some unchecked willful frenzy.
O to give comfort then!
To open oneself for Them to slake Their thirst!
But one must be pitiless.
One must then & ever
attempt to extricate oneself,
replace mystic consummation
with craft, simulation,
the textures of the terrestrial plane,
that the soul may come to find some degree of relief—
I do not say *cure*!—
from its devotion to glory,
if such relief be possible.

Sky

So we could remain caught between what we stand on that will not
  let us in,

& what falls down upon us, that will not let us go.

So we could have weather as a metaphor of the future.

So Chicken Little could run squawking off in search of rhyming
  poultry.

So there could be hailstones the size of golf balls, & so we could *say*
  they are the size of golf balls.

So small creatures blown to smithereens by various exploding
  substances from ACME

could have a place to spout up into, & sootily reassemble.

So James Dickey could make us watch his flight attendant fall

out of her crisp uniform & gauzy underwear all the way down.

So court astrologers could debate whether a comet was a *sign* or a
  cause of disaster.

So Constantine could behold against clouds the flaming monogram,

& order that standard formed of jewels and gold.

So Elijah could be taken up, & Elisha mourn him.

So Christ could ascend. And the Virgin.

So artists could paint the mandorla, vehicle of ascension,

light & elliptical or massive & weighty, lifted by angels.

So Jacob's ladder could rest propped up against it.

So Cyrus Reed Teed of Utica, N.Y., could renounce it: *To know*

of the earth's concavity is to know God. While to believe

in the earth's convexity is to deny Him & all His works.

So Charles Fort could document showers of snakes, frogs, &
  gudgeons, always from a ringingly clear sky,

as well as downpourings of a gelatinous substance which, he
   hypothesized,

makes up part of an earth-enclosing shell through whose puncture
   wounds we glimpse the outer light called *stars.*

So we could be abducted into it just when we were on the verge of
   losing hope.

Even from the first, with everything that was going to happen,
   didn't we deserve such a sky?

There is so much traffic up there, yet it unfurls swiftly from

the contracting pinhole pupil of the eye.

Paresthesia

I was born under the
sign of the spider, &
I recognize all who
are my kin by their
headaches & chronometric
incongruities; sensitivities
to barometric shifts;
untidy, directionless
nostalgias; weepings,
heavings, compulsions,
faintings & untimely
levitations; copious
sweats, languorous
fatigues; vertigo & visions
of coronas flaming out from
household appliances; episodes
of prophesy, aphasia,
amnesia, & spontaneous
bilocation—yet it is

by precision they
live, by *permutations &*
combination, the paths
of loneliness &
the preliminaries
of adhesion; they gauge
the currents whispering
across delicate
tactile hairs, they plot
radial & spiral, funnel

dome, doily & sheet still
liquid inside their
silk glands; they proceed
not by sight but by

vibration, Stradivari tasting
his glaze of tears, semen, blood
& other nameless holy & profane
secretions, that he might draw from
mute flamed maple the amber
flow of heart tones; James Hampton,
lone American awake in the
soporiferous fifties, stooping
among bulky blunt-faced
cars to retrieve gold & silver
aluminum foil, discarded
glass, plastic sheets, & wood scraps, each
treasure calling to him with its own voice or
voices so that as fiery
wings, eyes, seals, scales
lamps, & diadems, it might under his
hands in fullness of time rise up:
THE THRONE OF THE THIRD
HEAVEN OF THE NATIONS MILLENNIUM
GENERAL ASSEMBLY manifest
in glory!
Even Jonathan Edwards enumerating
in his soft dry voice the raptures
of hell, stood up in his day
to defend *pure sensation,*
inward, soul-animating—in this
I admit that it is he, not
his more humane but chillier
rationalist fellows, with whom I share

that spider rash on the invisible
underlining of the skin, burning,
mutating, travelling—oh,
there was spider milk
awash in the heavenly
cluster weaving through
nebulae faster than
thought on the eve of our
birth. And though several of my
legs are crumpled & there are
poisonous vapors in the wind,
though my exoskeleton
is cracked & one of my
sensilla punctured, I will
let out my line across not
an abyss of emptiness but rather
(worse!) great surges of possibility—

toward you
my life, my other, unseen
across space & time. On this
trembling, breath-
racked matrix of light
shimmering half
into disappearance, &
no sooner strung than
torn, I will
step out, yes,
& I will
walk!

Patron

I am the ceiling angel, a minor votary
              whose function is to catalogue, inspect,
& celebrate the ceilings of this world
              as each at its locus glorifies the Lord
in an admittedly outmoded fashion:
              the vast but strangely homey apparatus
of starry dome, concentric shells, empyrean,
              the chandelier the contractors dismantle,
each crystal dipped in clear cobalt solution,
              then lifted, dripping, to hover radiant
& soulless, trembling in its golden fixture;
              I have, I confess, a penchant for candelabra,
& quiver still with pleasure to remember
              how, before the days of fuse & wire,
the floating scent of beeswax filled the halls
              as, dancing on wicks the little flames rose up
steadfast & limber from their hearts of blue—
              once one, its moorings somehow loosened,
dropped from above, a blazing coronet,
              silent, accelerating as it fell.
To plummet burning, perfectly upright,
              transformed within the fraction of an instant
from marvel of design & calibration
              to splintered crystal fountain, glittering spray,
some hundred hanging hyperbolic arcs!—
              yes, the vacant space between floor & ceiling
exists to evoke the image of a fall
              from—what?—a painted heaven reproduced
for the elect in luminous mosaic?
              An imagined fall, perhaps of angels,

or of the dome itself, cracking, imploding
        like a robin's egg of sheerest blue
crushed by some passing indifference.
          Yet still the cut glass & precious stones refract
in blue & cinnabar the flickering light
        from lamps above the altars, barely swinging
against the shadowed marble & gold sheeting
        so that the entire hemisphere,
aglow & humming with the sacred chant,
        seems to rise swiftly through the deeper night.
These simultaneous opposing motions
        fall & ascent, both illusory,
make one light-headed—unless one is an angel,
        architecturally savvy, uninspired
by such effects. So many golden domes!
        I was relieved, I must admit, when later
the glass-skinned house was finally invented,
        London's Winter Garden, advertised
as *a veritable fairy land*—Victoria
        Herself inhaled the steamy air
surveyed the hydrocephalous roses,
        the hummingbirds shipped in at great expense,
& tilted back the heavy royal head
        to squint at the roof of glass flowing so slowly
it seemed quite still, though the truth is
        that a shattered pane, if left alone,
could in a million years grow back together,
        healing itself, as the Queen's heart
in widowhood would never learn to do.
        An edifice of marvellous intelligence,
She said for the following morning's *London Times,*
        an ambiguous remark, as if the Queen
wondered whether that intellect belonged
        to the building itself or to its engineers—

indeed, a ceiling does connote intelligence,
              as the first mud-roofed domes resembled
helmets—or skulls—the bony cranial socket
              which, like a beehive, houses the vibrations
of winged life, sentient & multivocal—
              therefore, the imagined rise & fall
must be of human thought, its old ambition
              & exquisite failure to transcend
the limits preordained by structure.
              Angels, like sharks, dream in continuous motion
Languorous, cruising these drafts & microcurrents,
              I dream the death of ceilings, the icy ether
of my own redundance: the American ceiling
              prophesied on nineteenth century canvasses
where light & air at once expand, dissolve—
              sky for thought to swim in unimpeded,
& Heaven set her starry crown aside.

December 31, 1999

If starships carrying the 33,000 Interplanetary Brethren do not touch
   down, scorching the tenderly sprayed & spritzed lawns of the
   Dallas suburbs; If the Fords, Chevrolets, & various other
   American-made vehicles of the elect do not careen into each other
   as their operators are plucked out, passing miraculously through
   the waxed & rust-proofed molecules of their chrome roofs to
   ascend into the scrolled-back sky without a single downward
   glance;

If California, Nevada, Oregon, Arizona, Idaho, Utah, Colorado, &
   Texas do not sink to rest under several thousand tons of ocean,
   as, some say, they have always richly deserved, unrecoverable yet
   unmourned due to the long-awaited rising of Atlantis in
   proximity to the spot where Florida is now, as revealed to
   Gordon-Michael Scallion, a former Floridian, in 29 nights of
   dreams after he "mysteriously lost his voice in the middle of a
   business meeting";

If the Antichrist, unanimously reported by astrologers to have been
   born in the early 1960s somewhere in the Middle East, & later
   educated at a prestigious Western university, fails to manifest
   himself & lead the world into a false & fatal peace in which it
   becomes apparent that our MasterCards & Visas have been, as
   we suspected all along, a trap disguising the power of 666, & yes,
   you *should* have cut them up that midnight you stood in the stark
   kitchen glare raving that you were finally going to *change your
   life,* but the next morning's flapjacks, nuked & stacked high with
   a dollop of whipped fake butter melting languidly on top, lulled
   you out of what you then decided was just an oddball mood;

If, despite weeping statues, sleeping prophets, faxes of doom, & the
   undisclosed revelation to the pope by the Blessed Virgin at

Fatima, the poles do not shift, the pyramids do not ignite & lift off, & the holy crusaders do not burst from their graves in full attire, riding their plumed horses across godless Europe like a single breaker curled & cresting, &, running naked before them, bearing their terrible standard, the lost babes of the Children's Crusade, the iron mills & almshouses of the Industrial Revolution, & the milk carton photos of an occluded generation, innocent, luminous, & wholly without mercy;

With what shall the soul be left?

The soul that stumbles both within & outside the body as if in a blind drunk, craving the totalitarian whiteout of some unmediated Absolute?

Only January's bleak gaze on the cut glass rays frozen in their centrifugal diffusion from a bullet hole in the windshield of a once creamy 1967 Buick sinking in a trash-strewn field amidst the muted browns, mauves, & grays of North American winter.

Only the tone music of the ice-lashed pylons on the old suspension bridge, bright net pulsating in the play of shudder & gust.

Only the silk oozing from Tegenaria the house spider's spinnerets as once again she repairs her crude & ragged sheet web, torn by the titanic struggle of a recent meal.

Yes, it is just past solstice, & nothing has ended after all, so the soul must abandon its natural hysteria, make do with what light it finds, even winter light with no warmth in it moving slowly over the artifacts of this world.

How else would you need to awaken?

Holes

There is no way to begin when speaking of holes,
except possibly by announcing that sometimes
I will use the abbreviation "h" instead of the actual word,
since, said too often, it starts to sound like
yodeling, an activity which in itself depends on holes,
the voice propelled through the throat & open mouth,
then hurtled back & forth across various local chasms rising
to distort it, as if the voice, aware that it is always full of holes,
wants to revel in hyperbole—why not celebrate
its unstable & internally spacious nature,
rather than always strain to fill the holes
with self-deprecations, snivelling disclaimers?
I've never yodeled, though I did see "The Sound of Music."
Give thanks to the body, tireless manufacturer of empty spaces, & also
to the soul, which would surely be at home in the kingdom of the
    sponge.
The song of my life must be a song of holes
nested, honeycombed, growing from inside out or outside in.
Dream holes, prismatic & migratory.
Holes undulant & flickering, parasitic holes, & the famous
white hole in time, my last known address, from which I am
    speaking now,
where you can find everything that has been declared *out of the question.*
Their gravity. Their varying magnitudes.
Their ecosystems, their temporal & spatial drift.
Points of entry, ports of departure, O needle's cold eye,
perturbation in sheerest blue.
Of all h's, the impure ones are the holiest,
that is, most sacred—those that refuse to maintain their structure,
breaking down, melting into each other even as they rise into being.

O the gelatinous sounds of bliss or grief leaking into the world!
But often, they won't leave the belly where they feel safe—
thus the invention of such h-aids as the rosary, sequence
of tiny bubble-universes, hollow beads, holdable holes
on time's slack string, just as everything the penitent can't speak
lies within, threaded & coiled, little globes of ice, frozen
pockets of information wholly inaccessible until
the first drawn-in prayer-breath thaws them to tears.
How much of the body lives outside the body;
how much of the soul lives outside the soul?
Maria of the Starry Crown. Blue Mother.
There are many things in my life to be sorry for.
This stubborn love of h's is not one of them.

Stitching the Bride

"'I demand a creature of another sex, but as hideous as myself...'"
—Mary Shelley, *Frankenstein*

And sleepless once when the needle slipped, he could not
say whether it pierced his hand or was at that moment
born from it, stitching her
even through his dreams, the knots
invisible, revelatory: asymmetrical
breasts, knuckles, eyelid flaps with their little fringe,
& she all the while coming nearer,
approaching with incalculable slowness
to join him in the fleshly sampler
where a seam invokes the soul.
He belongs to her.
He is either her mother or her only child.
Poised at the point of arrival,
she awaits the galvanic touch
with a formal hesitation the instant before
she will pour herself into the mold shaped for her,
open the eyes from inside—one green, one black—

though he forever howls now,
ripping the tufted hair rich from its yellow scalp
as the head lolls back where the flesh of the throat
should smooth to the clavicle,
splitting the soft mouth just
where she would have entered.

But she has come so far toward his waiting
she cannot stop:
with no body to rest in, she must expand,
fill the room, knowing her vastness
as beautiful, clear all the way through,
for she will still
be the bride, faithful yet,
she the composition of his weather
& their mutual speed
as he glides on bladed runners
across Gothic ice, pursuing
what has been chasing him for years & is only
nine-tenths of a globe behind,
flying with him through a needle's eye
of absolute cold into adherence: who now is
human, who lost, who the one
without name? He had his
favorites though they never knew. Nothing
you repent of ever repents of you.

Heavenly Bodies

Swathed in midwinter night on the 27th floor of hotel hospital,
I find myself hoping that Manhattan woman who recently rose over
  her condo,
sucked skyward by a silver cylinder hovering just over the bridge,
was dressed in her most liquid lingerie, so that even while tranced
or terrified, she could shimmer, an act of self-location
in a universe of lights, for if life is, as they say, *hard,*
it's because we're forever compelled not only to rise,
as I do each morning, swinging up from the bed
on jointed aluminum crutches, but to *rise & shine,*
& there is, yes, a certain cruelty in it, as if the soul is a fish
reeled up on a hook from its sleep through a hole in the ice
to glitter, burning in winter light,
for the hard truth is that it won't ever be over,
that all who descend are really always rising,
as the voice from memory's grave bespeaks the living world,
grieving, *A single green stalk curving up through my sternum
continually undoes my sleep!*—grieving,
The plait, the weave, the lamination & the sheen!—
& tonight even the snowflakes are sent back up
by surface winds into a tossed cloud-clotted sky
where the little lights feed on the larger lights
even as they're born of them into the expansion
of things as we know them,
things with their variable imperfections,
as in what used to be called *lampwork,* where the molten glass,
blown outward, bears with it all its flaws,
both those embedded & those newly generated on the flight
through incandescence: silica fleck, blister, air bubble,

each distortion forever its own center here
to reflect, refract, effulge, & glisten,
& this is what the trembling has been for,
the shaking, the heat & pressure from within,
everywhere bodies rising & shining
in merciless slowness while with broken indistinguishable sighs
we fly apart together, we fly apart.

Blessing Song

After, despite, because of, & through it all
I believe in the blessing, & here transcribe
for my listening audience a brief version
of its history in local planes
& habitations, beginning
not with the evolution
of angels, of which we know
nothing, though we see their
failed adaptions roosting
slack-jawed on high-tension wires,
but with the Israelites in the Bible picture
where they forever stoop, reaching
for manna the illustrators must have struggled
to imagine as they sketched something halfway between
cobwebs & wafers: lace doilies, perhaps, or children's
snowflakes cut from paper just this side
of transparency, easily torn, yet not torn, held
briefly between thumb & finger. From this early,
still comparatively crude version we learn
the lightness of blessing as it descends
like an indolence of feathers,
an insulation of down, or the dew
spangling Gideon's fleece for a sign
in those days when signs are still meaningful
(having not yet exceeded their quota
in the visible world, & thereafter moving
their headquarters into the heart,
a red-letter date perhaps still to come
in the biography of consciousness).

This lightness Brueghel beholds, being the first
of his nation to portray with flecks of paint
a fall of snow so weightless it seems
to lift off from the manger's circumambient glow.
Even politically questionable Frank Capra
dreams it & is awarded
"a Class III Citation of technical excellence
for the the development of movie snow, a mixture
of foamite, soap & water blown
through a wind machine." This is also why
you, listeners, taste
of salt, even if it has been
a long time since your tongue has known
yourself or the world that way.
So fine-grained now, the blessing, as if
pulverized, sifting from the pneumatic
chisel of the cathedral's
stone carver as she shapes hydrocephalic
bubble-headed monsters with thick
protruding tongues, slit ears, &
bony feathered claws to grip
buttress & balustrade where
mother & infant sit enthroned
in dim clouds of prayer.
Note also its inelectable motility,
as in spring, veils of gold
pollen float on the air, bridal,
sheer as the fragrance
of the sensimila stalk placed burning
in Bob Marley's casket. Nothing
exerts more force
than motion of drift though
crack or cranny,
than powder, ash so white it's

blue, the fall
from the body into
the body where there is a glory
around each blossom,
there is a nimbus
around the throne, made up of
dust, foam, smoke, all residue born by
the heart's varied winds:
periodic, constant, local, &
cyclonic. Either the little stories
are coalescing, or the one big story
is breaking down into song so silent
it won't leave you alone, & it starts
like this.

Credo

That refined cane sugar is not & has never been responsible for
hyperactivity, heart disease, or tooth decay,

& that I was aware of this fact long before the experts.

That it is virtually impossible to find a real job through the want ads.

That objects fall into a swoon at the human touch, though whether
in bliss or trauma, I do not know.

That in both cooking & romance, substitution is possible only
without guarantee.

That the Bureau of Omens has been downsized on account of its
outrageous electric bill.

That my little niece who during a family reunion escaped into the
kitchen to take one bite from each of 42 barbecued hot dogs
thereby undeniably demonstrated her already formidable life skills.

That the dream world is both spongier & more vitreous than can be
imagined.

That the energy within a resolution becomes available only as it is
broken.

That piety is wholly indigestible, even for God, especially for God.

That the lit wick, burning at one end & drowning at the other,
sings the only word it knows: *More!*

That the law of physics by which I flicker in & out of being
approximately a billion times a second
is an inconvenience but not, in fact, a problem,
God having been ever a sucker for any strobe.

That nearly everyone on this planet is fully qualified to be not only
the President of the Alliance for Twins Tragically Separated,
but a member as well.

That my vocation is to classify the varieties of breakage in this world
    & certain others.

That knowledge is a plume of gas bubbles without color or odor
seeping nearly undetectably from a hairline crack in the ocean floor.

No, it is light glinting from the glittering wings of a swarm passing
    too quickly to be identified.

Though I have never been a swan, I've been assured there is a swan
    in my future.
Even now from that mysterious downy tribe I send you greetings,
    O mortal kin,
from the soul's farthest outposts where stars tangle in the watery
    roots of weeds.

But what right have I to rise winged above the ranks of the
    bewildered & disfigured,
those who have only themselves to blame, but knowing this,
suffer no less acutely?

That to the extent I do escape, it is neither to my credit nor for my
    own salvation,

because we have been placed between the imperceptible & the
    unbearable,
the unforeseen & the irretrievable,

everything that irradiates us
& that which we so inveterately illumine,

all that has been hidden, brother,
& sister, all that has been revealed.

That there is only one prayer I am capable of saying, & it goes like
    this:

From my name today, which is so far Claire Bateman,

from my borrowed house in Tennessee, home of pawnshops,
    discount fireworks retail extravaganzas, mountains floating
    blue inches above the horizon, & the International
    Towing & Recovery Hall of Fame & Museum—O universal
    fantasy of timely rescue, permanent reprieve!—

from my stitched ribs,
my soul overflowing the skin's slack mesh,

the prosthetic museum of my limbs and vital organs,
the silicon chip implanted in my cerebellum,
& the steel plate in my tiny electrified skull,

on behalf of the entire food chain,

the unborn & the undead,

all mineral proliferation & vegetal excess,

from the alligator hatchlings wriggling into the heart's sewers

to the mystic physicians at Tech Support who hourly part the raging
    information sea that the chosen ones might, dry shod, pass through,

on behalf of the 13 sacred secretions,
most notably,

lard
honey
colostrum
& white swamp whiskey:

I am here to pronounce purgation
for creation's clogged arteries

that there may be an increase of delight in the world!

An increase of delight, I do now declare it,

& to this I dedicate myself,
for this I take responsibility,
be it either too heavy
or too devastatingly light.

That there is accumulation & breakdown,

clearing & occlusion,

coagulation & flow.

There is shaking & being shaken.

Friction

In the beginning, salve
without wound, the world
a swamp of unguents,
slick & ropy, rocked
in its own spume—
for ever so long

this was enough,
but the more she held it,
the more it seemed to demand—
what?—& as she pondered,
she felt it breaking down

in that grieving way,
as if it sought a form,
so she fashioned the bees
in whose waxy hives
it thickened into honey;
she dug out deep veins
for oil, secret
under the earth's skin;

she molded flesh
to contain it
in semen, saliva, tears;
by such slow leakage we measured
lifetime & plot line,
alluvial,

but that was not enough,
so she leaned down and whispered
to us, & we labored
at dark forge-flame so there were
valve and gear to grease—

it was hungry
for friction; it deserved
satisfaction, that even metals
might have their own
embodied heat, & that strangers
might finally meet,
touch and slide off

one another, glistening,
almost intact.
In the beginning
only lubrication,
& from it, love deduced
everything else.

About the Author

CLAIRE BATEMAN grew up in the Washington D.C. area and has lived in Ohio, Wisconsin, and Tidewater Virginia. She now lives in Greenville, South Carolina where she teaches creative writing at the Fine Arts Center, a magnet high school. She received a B.A. from Kenyon College in 1978 and an M.F.A. from Vermont College in 1993. She has won the Louisiana Literature Poetry Prize, the Brittingham Prize for Poetry, the New Millennium Writings Poetry Award, and was a finalist for the Walt Whitman Award. Her work has earned her grants from the National Endowment for the Arts and the Tennessee State Arts Commission. Her first book of poetry, *The Bicycle Slow Race*, was published by Wesleyan in 1991; *At the Funeral of the Ether* was published by Ninety-Six Press in 1998.

About the Cover Artist

MARY JOSEPHSON has exhibited her paintings since the early 1980s. She studied in Paris at the École National Superior des Beaux Arts before receiving a B.F.A. from the Pacific Northwest College of Art. Her work has been shown at the Portland Art Museum, the Oregon Health Sciences University, the University of Austin, Texas, and the Bellevue Art Museum in Washington. Prominent collections include Microsoft, Oregon State University, and the Portland Art Museum. She lives in Portland, Oregon where she is represented by the Laura Russo Gallery.